MW00804201

ADULT ALL-IN-ONE COURSE
Merry Christmas Book

Dennis Alexander

EASY SOLO ARRANGEMENTS WITH OPTIONAL DUET ACCOMPANIMENTS

This collection of favorite Christmas carols is the perfect supplement for adult beginners who are looking for easy solo arrangements with optional duet accompaniments that can be played by a more accomplished pianist. Both solo and duet parts have measure numbers for easy reference. Although each arrangement has been carefully written to conform to the technical and musical concepts of the Alfred All-In-One Course, students using any adult method will find these carols enjoyable and satisfying to learn and play. Best wishes for a very happy, musical and merry Christmas season!

Dennis Alexander

Christmas lights photo: © 1997 PhotoDisc, Inc.
Piano photo: Jeff Oshiro

Away in a Manger

Rev. Martin Luther
James E. Spilman
Arr. by Dennis Alexander

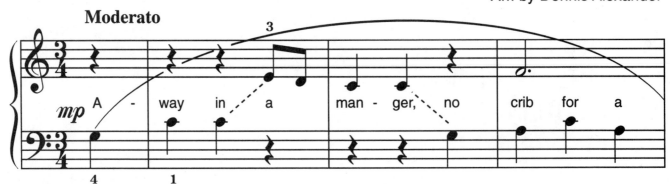

OPTIONAL DUET PART (Student plays 1 octave higher.)

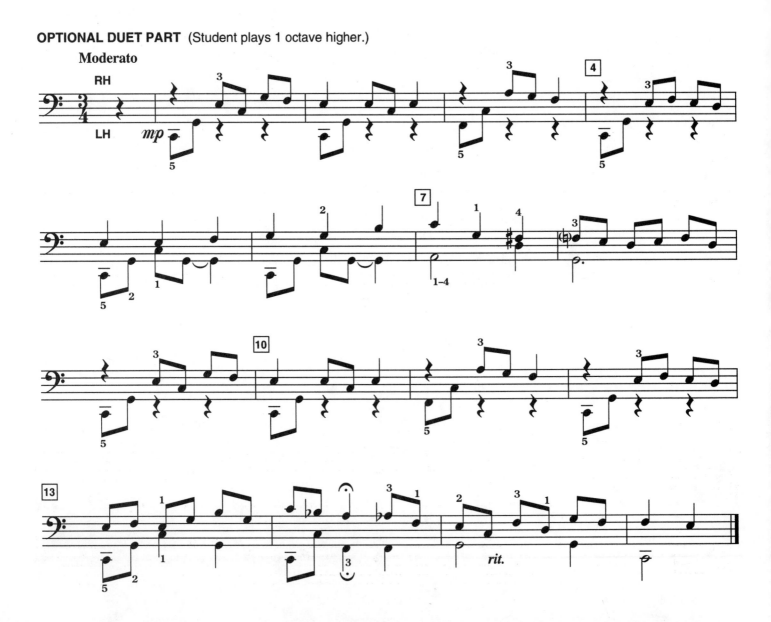

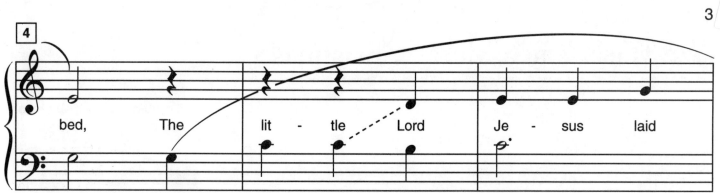

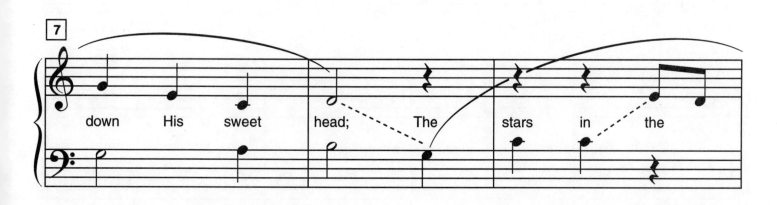

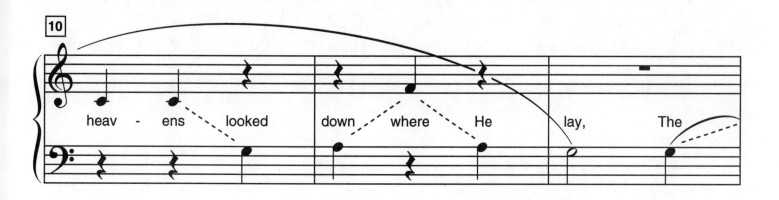

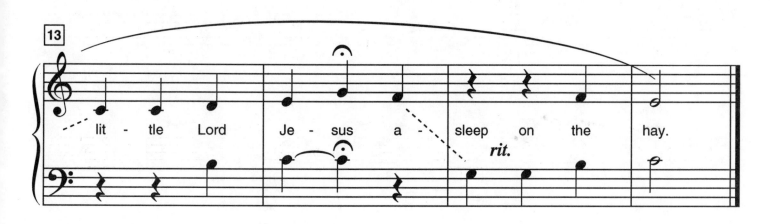

We Wish You a Merry Christmas

Traditional English Carol
Arr. by Dennis Alexander

OPTIONAL DUET PART (Student plays 1 octave higher.)

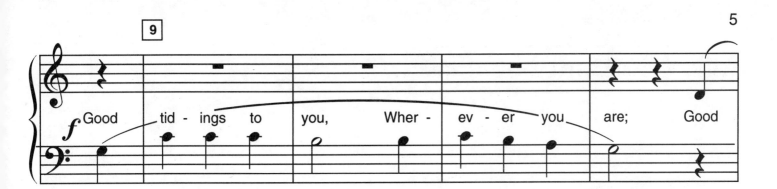

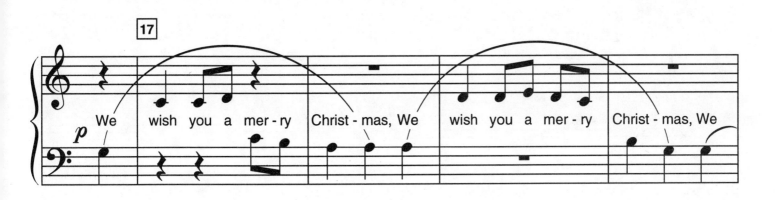

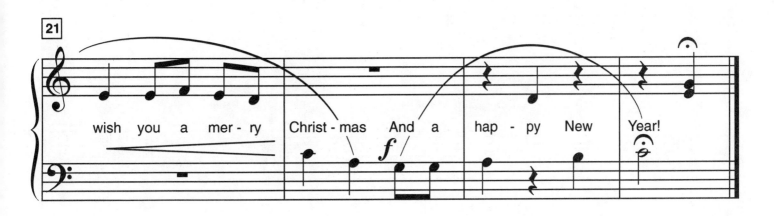

Jolly Old Saint Nicholas

Traditional Carol
Arr. by Dennis Alexander

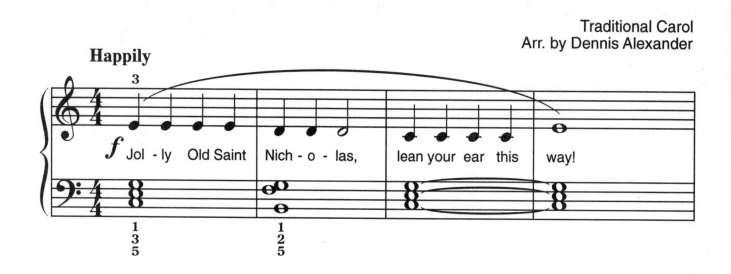

OPTIONAL DUET PART (Student plays 1 octave higher.)

Don't you tell a sin - gle soul what I'm going to say;

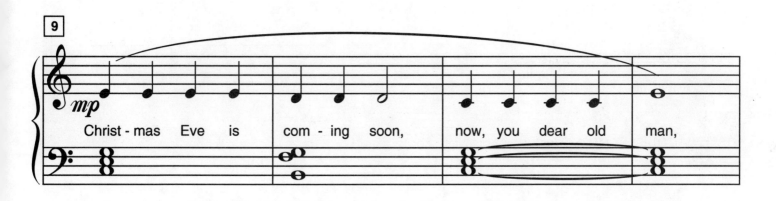

mp

Christ - mas Eve is com - ing soon, now, you dear old man,

Whis - per what you'll bring to me, tell me if you can.

rit.

We Three Kings of Orient Are

Words and music by John Henry Hopkins
Arr. by Dennis Alexander

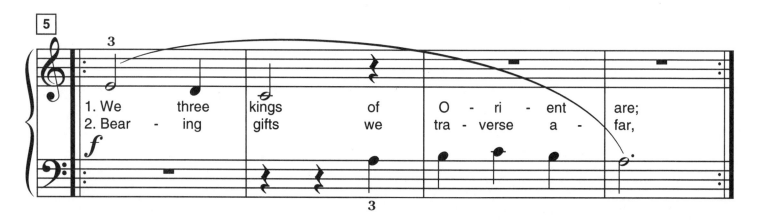

OPTIONAL DUET PART (Student plays 1 octave higher.)

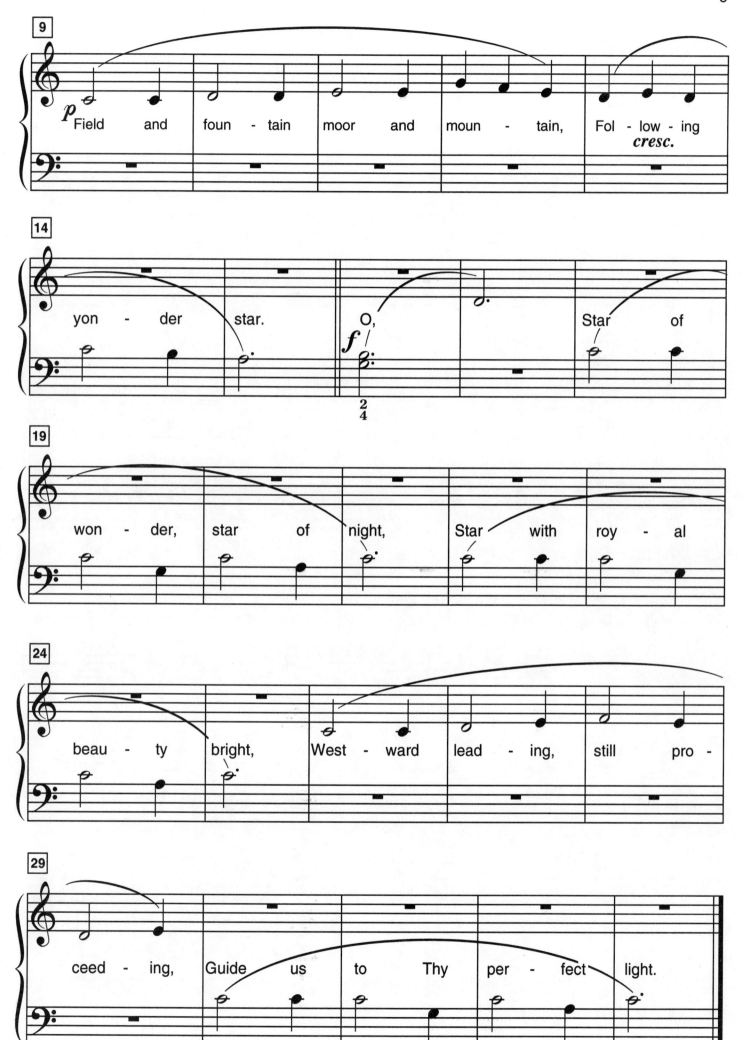

Silent Night

Words by Joseph Mohr

Music by Franz Grüber
Arr. by Dennis Alexander

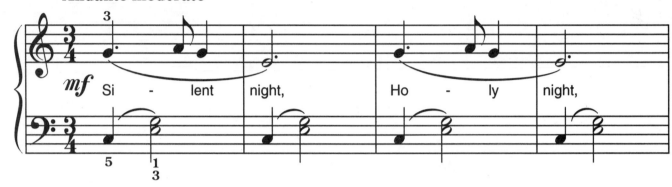

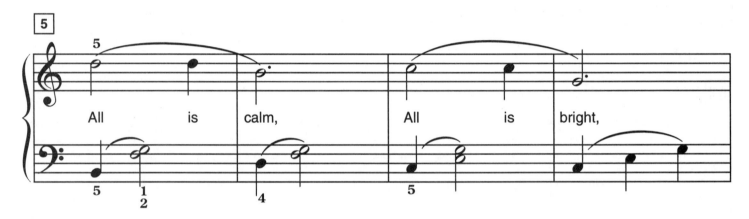

OPTIONAL DUET PART (Student plays 1 octave higher.)

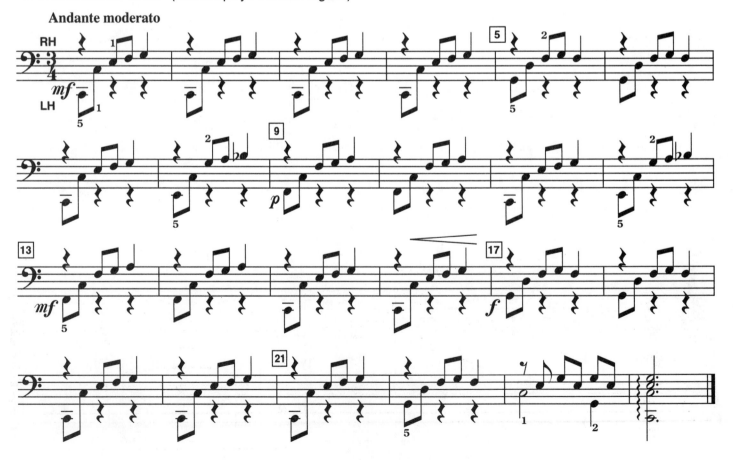

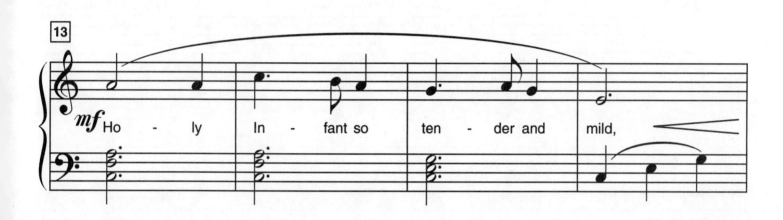

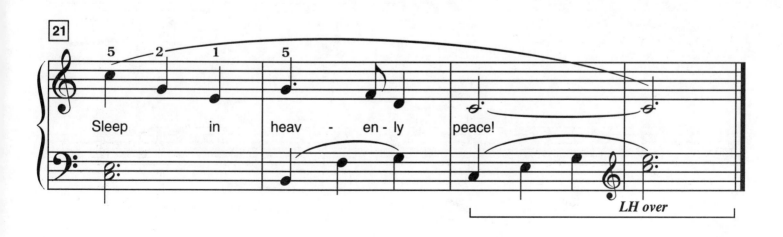

LH over

Deck the Halls

Welsh Carol
Arr. by Dennis Alexander

Deck the halls with boughs of hol - ly, Fa la la la la, la la la la,

OPTIONAL DUET PART (Student plays 1 octave higher.)

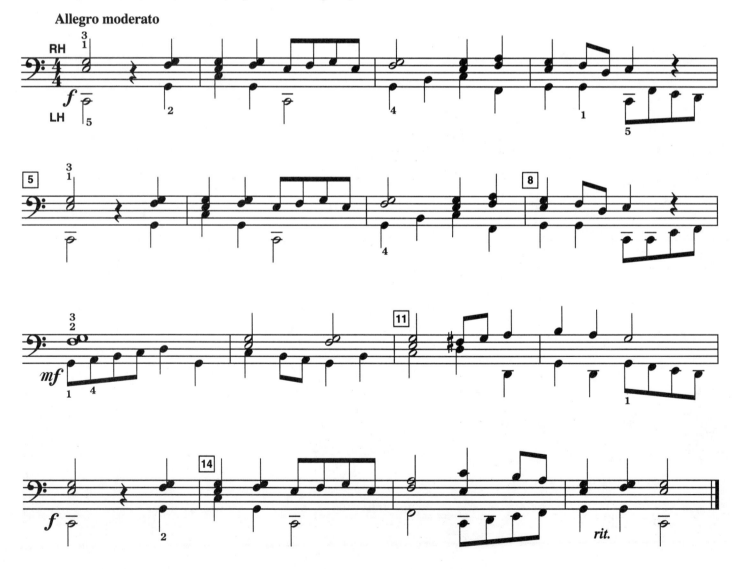

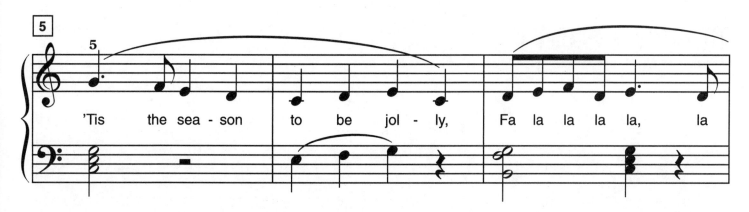

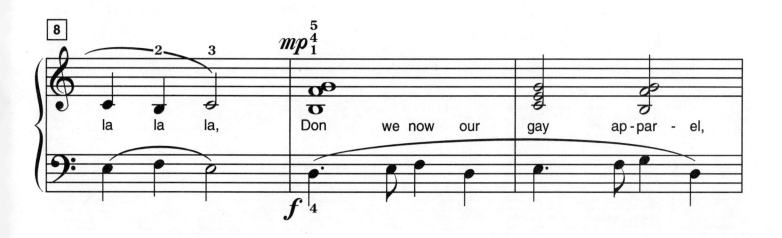

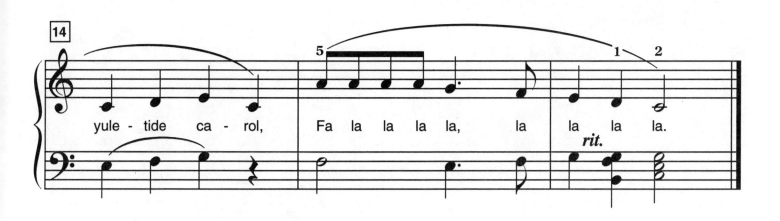

The First Noel

Traditional English Carol
Arr. by Dennis Alexander

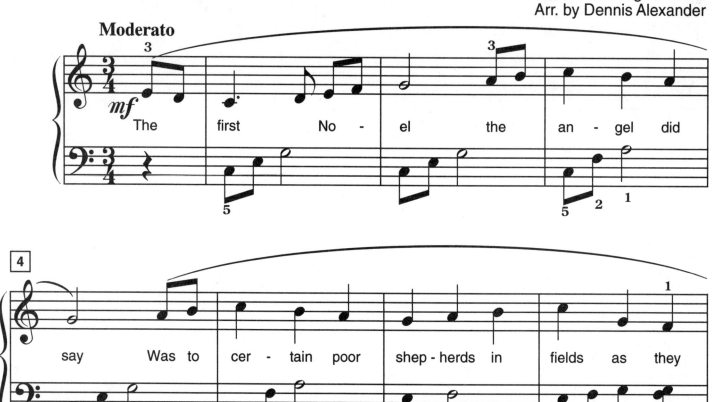

The first No - el the an - gel did

say Was to cer - tain poor shep - herds in fields as they

OPTIONAL DUET PART (Student plays 1 octave higher.)

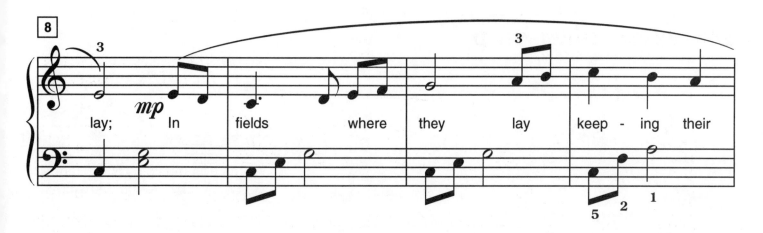

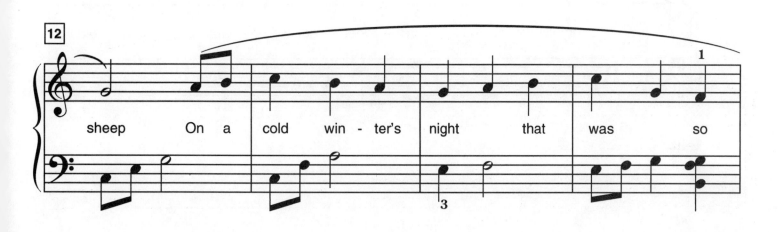

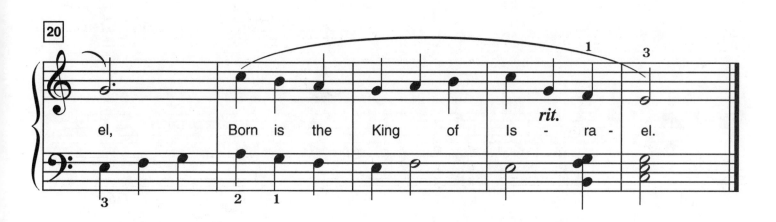

Up on the Housetop

Words and music by B.R. Hanby
Arr. by Dennis Alexander

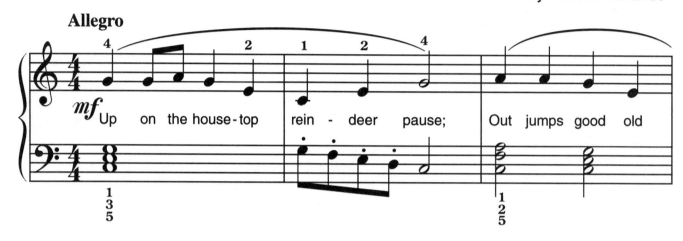

Up on the house-top rein - deer pause; Out jumps good old

OPTIONAL DUET PART (Student plays 1 octave higher.)

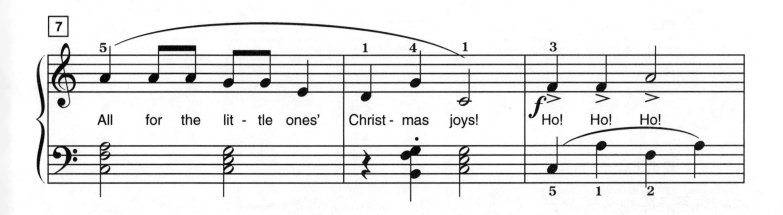

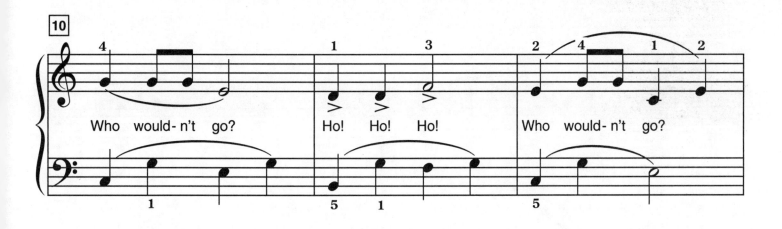

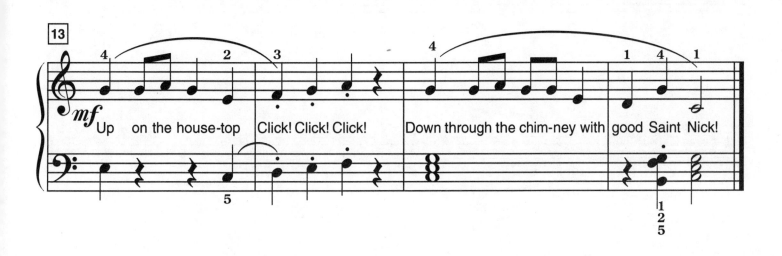

Hark! The Herald Angels Sing

Words by Charles Wesley

Music by Felix Mendelssohn
Arr. by Dennis Alexander

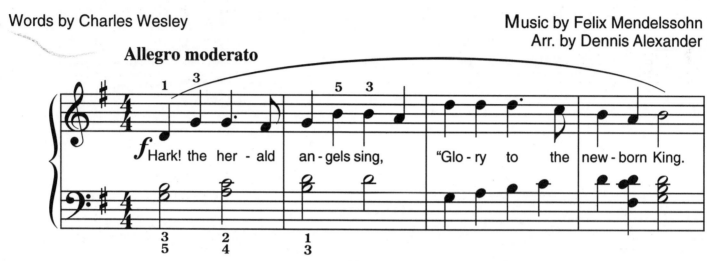

Hark! the her - ald an - gels sing, "Glo - ry to the new - born King.

OPTIONAL DUET PART (Student plays 1 octave higher.)

Allegro moderato

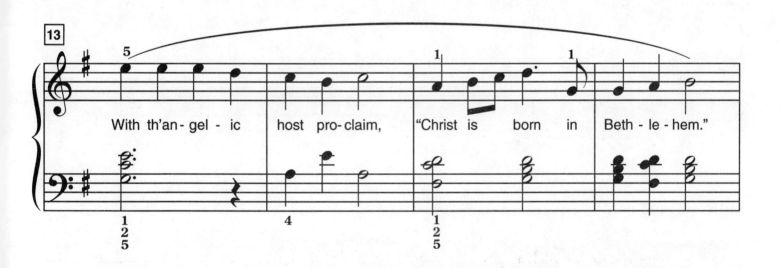

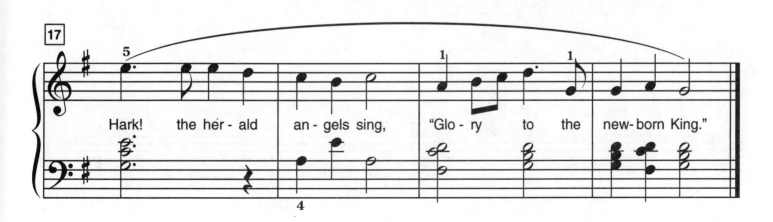

Once in Royal David's City

Words by Cecil F. Alexander

Music by Henry J. Gauntlett
Arr. by Dennis Alexander

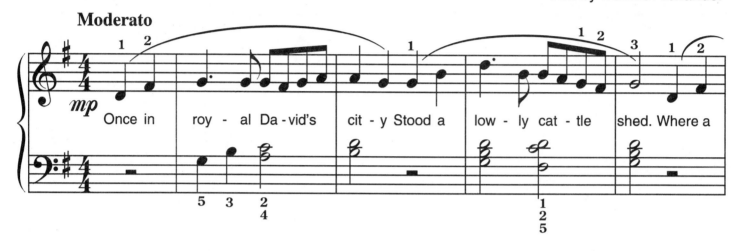

Once in roy - al Da - vid's cit - y Stood a low - ly cat - tle shed. Where a

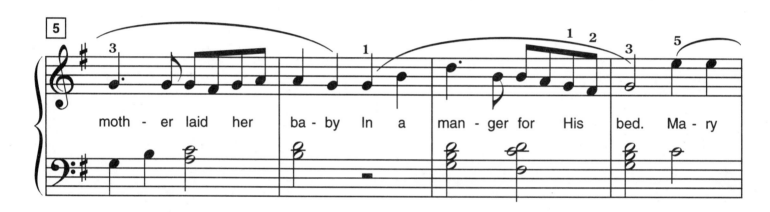

moth - er laid her ba - by In a man - ger for His bed. Ma - ry

OPTIONAL DUET PART (Student plays 1 octave higher.)

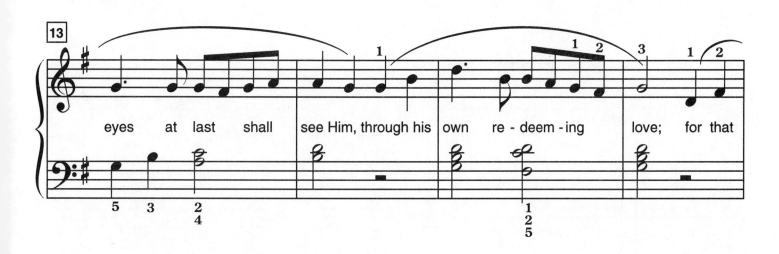

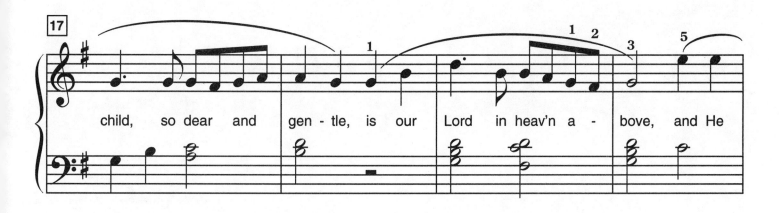

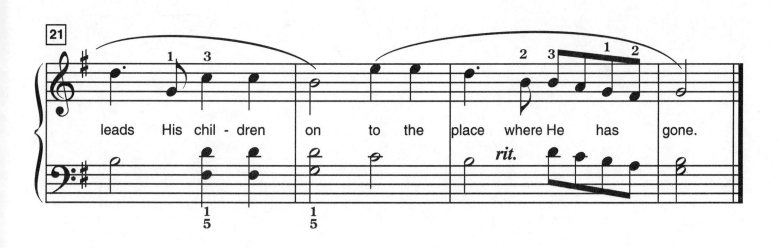

What Child Is This?

Old English Melody
Arr. by Dennis Alexander

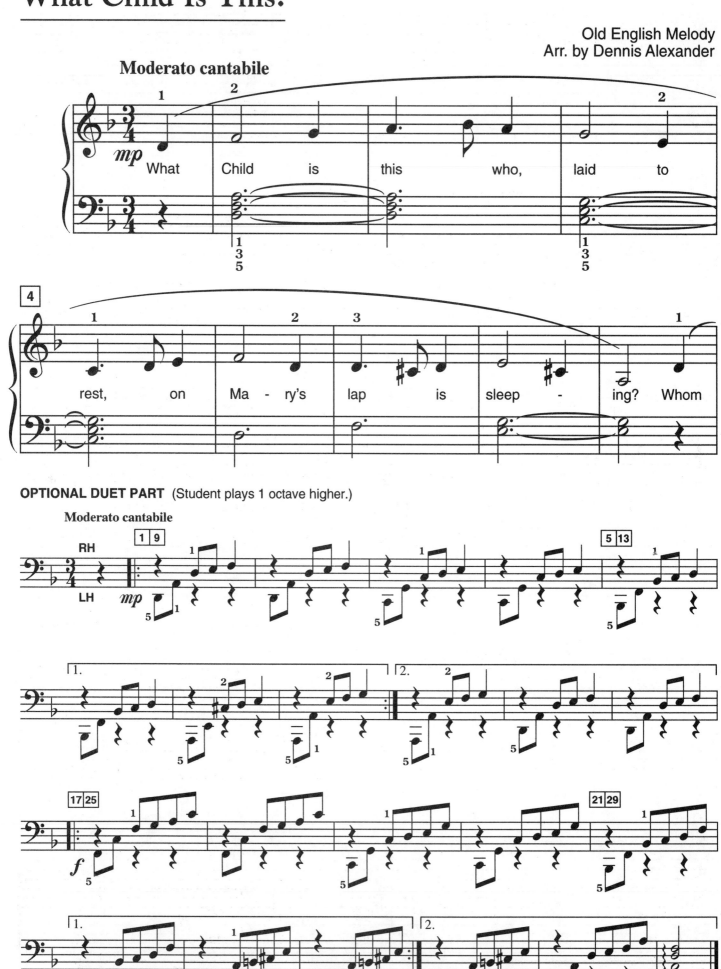

OPTIONAL DUET PART (Student plays 1 octave higher.)

O Christmas Tree

Traditional German Carol
Arr. by Dennis Alexander

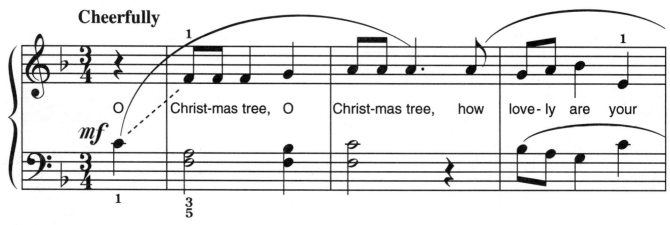

O Christ-mas tree, O Christ-mas tree, how love-ly are your

OPTIONAL DUET PART (Student plays 1 octave higher.)

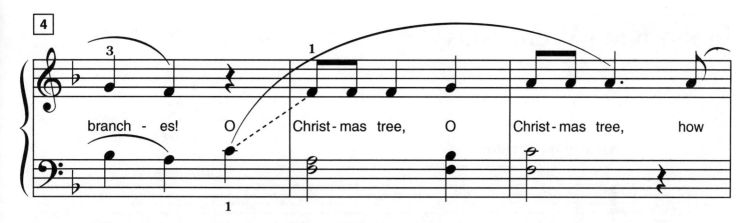

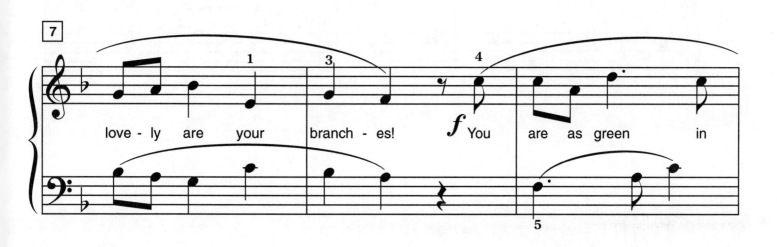

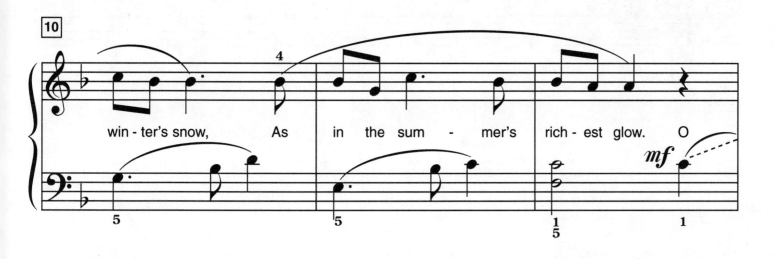

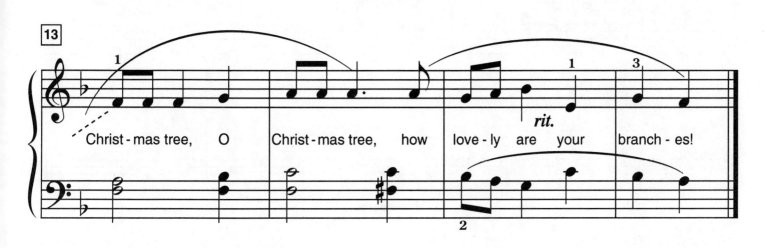

Good King Wenceslas

Traditional English Carol
Arr. by Dennis Alexander

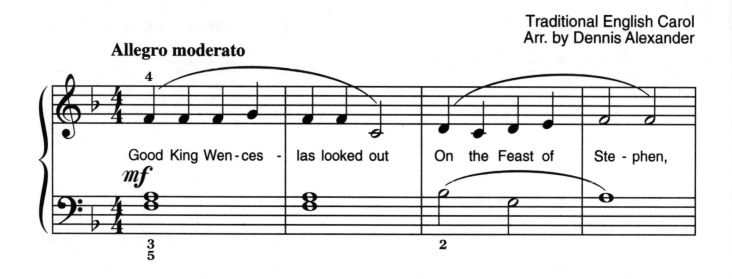

Good King Wen - ces - las looked out | On the Feast of | Ste - phen,

OPTIONAL DUET PART (Student plays 1 octave higher.)

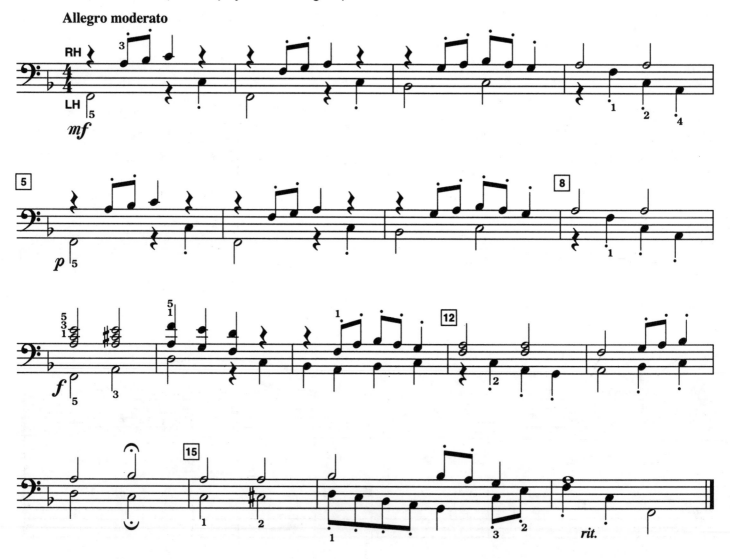

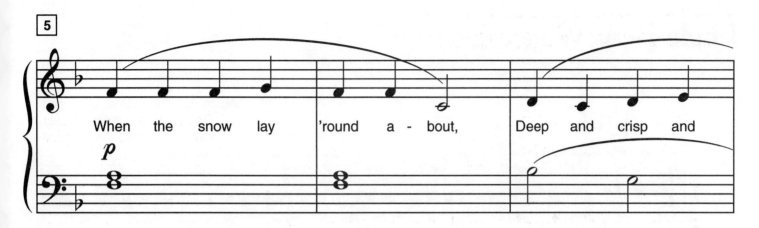

When the snow lay 'round a - bout, Deep and crisp and

e - ven. Bright - ly shone the moon that night, Though the frost was

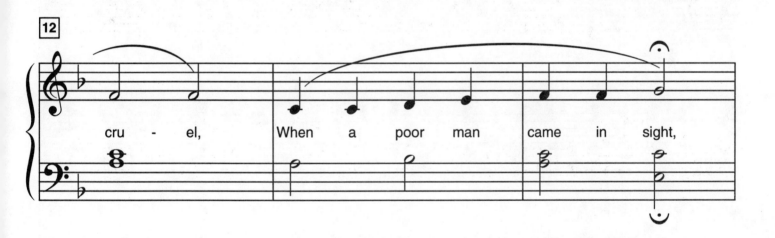

cru - el, When a poor man came in sight,

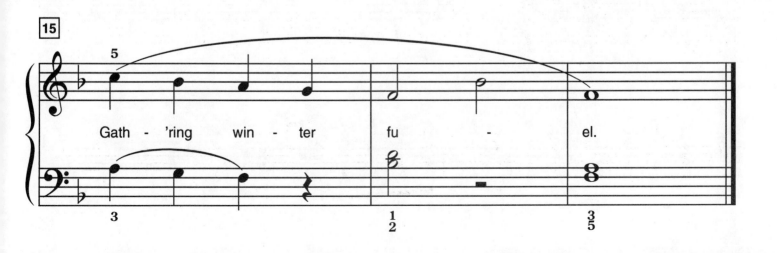

Gath - 'ring win - ter fu - el.

Jingle Bells

Words and music by James Pierpont
Arr. by Dennis Alexander

OPTIONAL DUET PART (Student plays 1 octave higher.)

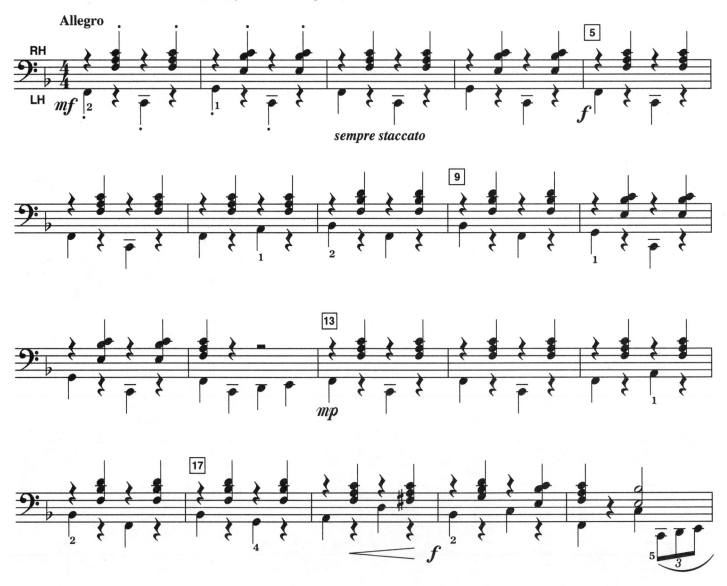

5
f Dash-ing through the snow in a one-horse o-pen sleigh,

9
O'er the fields we go, Laugh-ing all the way;

13
mp Bells on bob-tail ring, Mak-ing spir-its bright, What

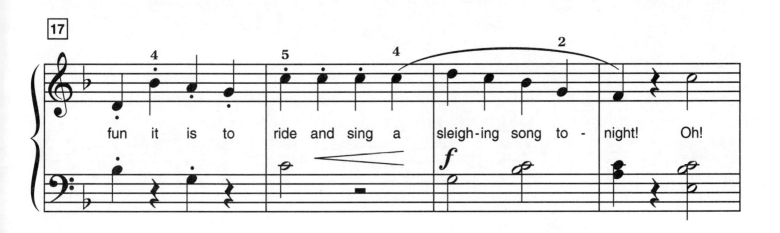

17
fun it is to ride and sing a sleigh-ing song to - night! Oh!

Jin - gle bells! Jin - gle bells! Jin - gle all the way!

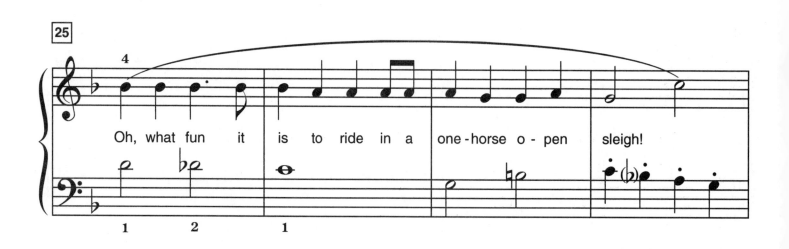

Oh, what fun it is to ride in a one - horse o - pen sleigh!

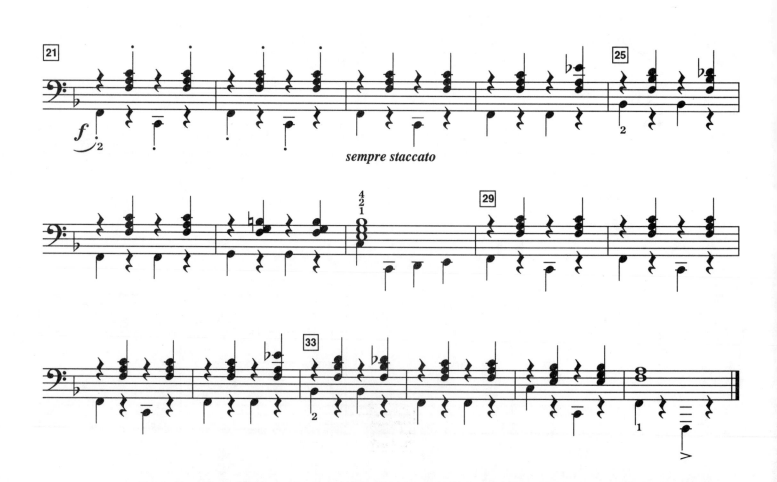

sempre staccato

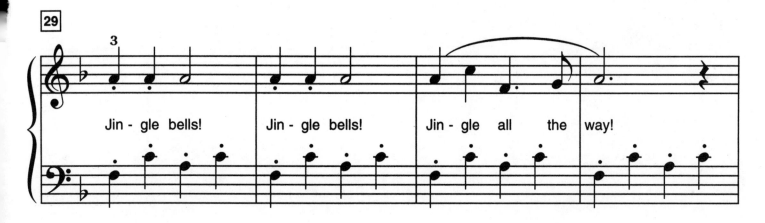

Jin - gle bells! Jin - gle bells! Jin - gle all the way!

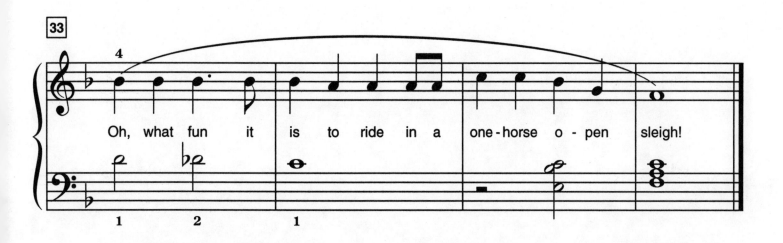

Oh, what fun it is to ride in a one - horse o - pen sleigh!